SURINAME 2016 HUMAN RIGHTS REPORT

EXECUTIVE SUMMARY

Suriname is a constitutional democracy with a president elected by the unicameral National Assembly. Elections for the National Assembly took place in May 2015, and in July 2015 the Assembly elected Desire Delano Bouterse to a second consecutive term as president. International observers considered legislative elections to be free and fair.

Civilian authorities maintained effective control over the security forces.

The most serious human rights problem was the unresolved trial of President Bouterse and 21 codefendants for the 1982 extrajudicial killings of 15 political opponents. There was concern about judicial independence because the executive and legislative branches delayed and otherwise interfered with progress toward a verdict in this high-profile case.

Other human rights problems included: poor conditions in detention centers; self-censorship by media organizations and journalists; widespread government corruption; violence and abuse against women and children; trafficking in persons; continued lack of recognition of land rights for indigenous and tribal peoples; discrimination against lesbian, gay, bisexual, transgender, and intersex persons and other minorities; and child labor in the informal sector.

The government took steps to investigate, prosecute, and punish officials who committed violations, whether in the security forces or elsewhere in the government. Observers nonetheless expressed concern that high public officials and security officers had impunity from enforcement.

Section 1. Respect for the Integrity of the Person, Including Freedom from:

a. Arbitrary Deprivation of Life and other Unlawful or Politically Motivated Killings

There were no reports that the government or its agents committed arbitrary or unlawful killings during the year. Authorities investigated all killings by police and security force members. Little information was available about investigations into killings by police or other security force members.

In October the minister of justice and police confirmed that nine police officers used excessive force in the 2012 shooting and killing of four unarmed men. At year's end authorities continued to investigate the circumstances of the case. Earlier in the year, Allied Collective, a local human rights organization, took the case to the Inter-American Commission on Human Rights (IACHR) for investigation of the circumstances surrounding the deaths, and in August the government reported that it had submitted a response to a request from the IACHR concerning details of the case.

There were developments in the trial of former military dictator and current President Bouterse and 21 codefendants for the 1982 extrajudicial killing of 15 political opponents. Following the November 2015 ruling of the Court of Justice to resume the trial, the prosecution requested that the court-martial continue to suspend trial proceedings. (The killings took place during a period of military dictatorship, and the majority of defendants were military.) In early June the court-martial lifted the suspension and continued trial proceedings from the point at which they were suspended in 2012, after arguing that authorities had made no notable progress to resolve the constitutionality of the 2012 Amnesty Law and that a four-year suspension of trial proceedings violated reasonable limits. Given the continued absence of a constitutional court (which is required by the constitution but has never been established), the court-martial made use of its own constitutional mandate and ruled that the Amnesty Law did in fact infringe on a trial in progress. The court-martial also dismissed the cases against the three deceased defendants.

In June, as the prosecutor prepared to deliver closing remarks and a sentencing recommendation in the case, the government invoked Article 148 of the constitution, which allows the government to order the attorney general to cease further prosecution of all suspects in the trial as a matter of state security. Based on instructions in the resolution, the prosecutor asked the court-martial to end the proceedings formally. The court-martial was scheduled to issue its ruling in January 2017.

There was no progress made on establishing the Truth and Reconciliation Commission as mandated by the Amnesty Law.

b. Disappearance

There were no reports of politically motivated disappearances.

c. Torture and Other Cruel, Inhuman, or Degrading Treatment or Punishment

While the law prohibits such practices, human rights groups, defense attorneys, and media continued to report instances of mistreatment by police, including unnecessary use of force during arrests and beatings while in detention.

There was a report of three prison guards beating a prisoner after the prisoner reportedly tampered with the electrical wiring of his cell, causing serious injury to a fourth guard. The case remained under investigation.

Prison and Detention Center Conditions

Prison conditions generally met international standards, but there were numerous problems in the country's 26 detention centers.

Physical Conditions: In prisons there were no major reports of conditions that raised human rights concerns. Nonetheless, prisons were understaffed, with high prisoner-to-guard ratios. Facilities lacked adequate emergency exits. Cells were closed with individual padlocks, and there were no emergency evacuation drills.

Overcrowding was a problem in the detention centers operated by police. Older buildings lacked adequate lighting and ventilation, with limited functioning sanitation facilities. Hygienic conditions were poor. Bad drainage led to flooding problems in some facilities.

Police have no standard operating procedures for management of detention facilities. Each facility has its own rules. Police officers were assigned to detention facilities without any specialized training. Facilities lacked adequate guards, relying instead on regular duty police officers when additional assistance is necessary. Officers did not have adequate medical protective gear to handle detainees in need of medical attention. There were reported cases of communicable diseases in detention facilities.

Outside vendors were responsible for providing food. Throughout the year vendors threatened to suspend services due to lack of payment by the government.

Administration: No ombudsman served on behalf of prisoners and detainees. Authorities investigated credible allegations of inhuman conditions. Government officials continued regular monitoring of prison and detention center conditions.

<u>Independent Monitoring</u>: The government permitted monitoring visits by independent human rights observers.

d. Arbitrary Arrest or Detention

The law prohibits arbitrary arrest and detention, and the government generally observed these prohibitions.

Role of the Police and Security Apparatus

The armed forces are responsible for national security and border control, with the military police having direct responsibility for immigration control at the country's ports of entry. All elements of the military are under the control of the Ministry of Defense. Civilian police bear primary responsibility for the maintenance of law and order and report to the Ministry of Justice and Police. Police effectiveness was hampered by a lack of equipment and training and by low salaries. Police and military continued to conduct regular joint patrols as part of the government's overall efforts to combat crime, and both also served on special security teams.

Civilian authorities maintained effective control over the military and police. Although the government continued to take steps to prosecute abusers in the security forces, observers nonetheless expressed concern that high public officials and security officers had impunity from enforcement.

The Personnel Investigation Department (OPZ), an office within the Police Department, investigated complaints filed by citizens against members of the police force. The Internal Affairs Unit (ITZ) investigated allegations of misconduct by members of the police force. Military police and the judge advocate investigated offenses committed by soldiers.

As of September the OPZ received 94 complaints from private citizens against members of the police force, nine of which contained allegations of abuse. By the same date, the ITZ had investigated 238 cases involving various forms of misconduct. Authorities imposed disciplinary sanctions in 223 cases, of which 15 included terminations from duty; other terminations were pending.

Arrest Procedures and Treatment of Detainees

Police apprehended individuals openly with warrants based on sufficient evidence and brought them before an independent judiciary. The law provides that detainees be brought before a judge within seven days to determine the legality of their arrest. Authorities promptly informed detainees of the charges against them. An assistant district attorney or a police inspector may authorize incommunicado detention. If additional time is needed to investigate the charge, a judge may extend the detention period for periods of 30 days, up to a total of 150 days. There is no bail system. Release pending trial is dependent on the type of crime committed and the judge handling the case. Detainees received prompt access to counsel of their choosing, but the prosecutor may prohibit access if the prosecutor believes access could harm the investigation. Legal counsel was provided at no charge for indigent detainees. Detainees were allowed weekly visits from family members.

Detainee's Ability to Challenge Lawfulness of Detention before a Court: Detainees have the ability to challenge in court the legal basis or arbitrary nature of their detention and obtain prompt release and compensation if found to have been unlawfully detained.

e. Denial of Fair Public Trial

While the constitution provides for an independent judiciary, the unresolved trial of former military dictator and current President Bouterse and 21 codefendants suggested a lack of independence in practice (see section 1.a.). The executive used legal maneuvers to delay, if not terminate, criminal proceedings against Bouterse and codefendants.

Human rights activists complained that there is no effective remedy for constitutional violations, as a succession of governments failed to install a constitutional court as mandated by the constitution.

The dependence of the courts on the Ministry of Justice and Police and Ministry of Finance, both executive agencies, for funding called judicial independence into question. The interim president of the Court of Justice stated during the opening ceremony for the new session in October that this financial dependence negatively influenced the functioning of the judiciary.

According to the interim president of the Court of Justice, the country had only 19 of the 45 judges needed for the proper functioning of the judicial system. Due to a shortage of judges, prisoners who appealed their cases often served their full sentences before completion of lengthy appeals.

The judiciary lacked sufficient professional court managers and case management systems to oversee the courts' administrative functions and also lacked adequate physical space, factors that contributed to a significant case backlog. The judiciary made some progress in the timely processing of criminal cases, although the processing of civil cases continued to lag.

Trial Procedures

The law provides for the right to a fair public trial without undue delay in which defendants have the right to counsel, and the judiciary generally enforced this right. There were court-assigned attorneys for both the civil and penal systems. All trials are public except for indecency offenses and offenses involving children. Defendants enjoy a presumption of innocence and have the right to appeal. Defendants have the right to be present and to consult an attorney in a timely manner. Defendants and their attorneys have access to government-held evidence. Defendants' attorneys can question witnesses and present witnesses and evidence on the defendant's behalf. The courts assign private-sector lawyers to defend indigent detainees. If necessary, free interpretation is also provided. The law extends the above rights to all defendants. The law protects the names of the accused, and authorities do not release those names to the public or the media prior to conviction.

Legal assistance to indigent detainees continued to come under pressure as lawyers threatened to cease legal assistance due to lack of payment by the government. Cases concerning non-Dutch-speaking detainees were postponed on numerous occasions as interpreters suspended their services to the court due to a backlog in payments by the government. There was no notable progress during the year to alleviate these problems.

There are parallel military and civilian court systems, and military personnel generally are not subject to civilian criminal law. The military courts follow the same rules of procedure as the civil courts. There is no appeal from the military to the civil system.

Political Prisoners and Detainees

There were no reports of political prisoners or detainees.

Civil Judicial Procedures and Remedies

Individuals or organizations have the right to seek civil remedies for human rights violations in local courts. Individuals and organizations have the right to appeal decisions to regional human rights bodies; most cases are brought to the IACHR. The Inter-American Court for Human Rights has ruled against the country in several cases, but government enforcement of court rulings has been selective and sporadic.

f. Arbitrary or Unlawful Interference with Privacy, Family, Home, or Correspondence

The law prohibits such actions, and there were no reports that the government failed to respect these prohibitions. The law requires search warrants issued by quasi-judicial officers who supervise criminal investigations.

Section 2. Respect for Civil Liberties, Including:

a. Freedom of Speech and Press

The law provides for freedom of speech and press. Multiple media outlets published material critical of the government. An independent press, an effective judiciary, and a functioning democratic political system helped to promote freedom of speech and press.

<u>Violence and Harassment</u>: Journalists reported intimidation by government and nongovernment actors.

<u>Censorship or Content Restrictions</u>: Media members reported continued self-censorship in response to alleged pressure from government officials or government-affiliated entities on journalists who published negative stories about the administration. Nonetheless, the press carried articles critical of the government on a daily basis. In addition, many news outlets retained affiliations with particular political parties that could bias reporting. The generally low wages for journalists made them vulnerable to bias and influence, which further jeopardized the credibility of reporting. At state-owned media outlets, journalists reported attempts to influence the content of their reporting.

Nongovernmental organizations (NGOs) reported the selective awarding of advertising by the government.

Libel/Slander Laws: The country's criminal-defamation laws carry harsh penalties, with prison terms between three months and seven years. The harshest penalty is for expressing public enmity, hatred, or contempt towards the government.

Internet Freedom

There were no government restrictions on access to the internet, and the government asserted that it did not monitor private online communications without appropriate legal oversight. Nevertheless, journalists, members of the political opposition and their supporters, and other independent entities perceived government interference or oversight of e-mail and social media accounts. Internet access was common and widely available in the major cities but less common in remote areas, with limited bandwidth and often limited or no access to electricity. According to the International Telecommunication Union, 42 percent of citizens used the internet in 2015.

Academic Freedom and Cultural Events

There were no government restrictions on academic freedom or cultural events.

b. Freedom of Peaceful Assembly and Association

The law provides for the freedoms of assembly and association, and the government mostly respected these rights.

Freedom of Assembly

The constitution protects the freedom of assembly, and this right was respected in most cases. The "We are Tired" Movement, a domestic NGO that frequently protested government policy, was reportedly summoned by the district commissioner and required to obtain a permit to organize its rallies. This permit placed various restrictions on the group's protests. The same organization was denied a permit for a silent march supporting rule of law and protesting against what it considered to be attacks on the legal system. While security forces tried to stop marching protesters by lining up and forming a barricade, the march took place on August 5 without violence.

Freedom of Association

The law protects the right to freedom of association, and the government generally respected this right.

c. Freedom of Religion

See the Department of State's *International Religious Freedom Report* at www.state.gov/religiousfreedomreport/.

d. Freedom of Movement, Internally Displaced Persons, Protection of Refugees, and Stateless Persons

The constitution provides for freedom of internal movement, foreign travel, emigration, and repatriation. The government generally respected these rights.

Protection of Refugees

Access to Asylum: The country is guided by the 1951 Convention relating to the Status of Refugees and its related Protocol. Thus the country relies on the Office of the UN High Commissioner for Refugees (UNHCR) to assign refugee or asylum seeker status. Once status has been confirmed, refugees or asylum seekers obtain residency permits under the country's Alien Legislation law.

In 2015 the Red Cross Suriname became the local point of contact for those filing for refugee status with UNHCR.

Stateless Persons

A 2014 amendment to the Citizenship and Residency Law grants citizenship through place of birth to a child who is born in the country to non-Surinamese parents, but who does not automatically acquire citizenship of one of the parents. The amended law aims to eliminate the possibility of statelessness among children but does not apply retroactively, so a person born before September 2014 continues to be subject to the old citizenship rules. Thus, children born before September 2014 in undocumented Brazilian-national mining communities or to foreign women in prostitution become eligible to apply for citizenship only at the age of 18. Unless paid for privately, these children are not eligible for government services such as education and health care.

Section 3. Freedom to Participate in the Political Process

The law provides citizens the ability to choose their government in free and fair periodic elections held by secret ballot and based on universal and equal suffrage.

Elections and Political Participation

<u>Recent Elections</u>: The constitution provides for direct election of the 51-member National Assembly no later than five years after the prior election date. The National Assembly in turn elects the president by a two-thirds majority vote. After legislative elections in May 2015, the National Assembly re-elected Desire Bouterse as president in July 2015. Observers from the Organization of American States and the Union of South American States judged that the elections were well organized and generally free and fair.

<u>Participation of Women and Minorities</u>: No laws limit political participation of women and minorities in the political process, and women and minorities did so. Four of the 17 cabinet ministers are women, as are 14 of the 51 members of the National Assembly.

Section 4. Corruption and Lack of Transparency in Government

Although the law provides criminal penalties for official corruption, the government did not implement the law effectively. There were numerous reports of government corruption, but no cases came to trial during the year.

<u>Corruption</u>: Allegations of corruption grew more prevalent as the economy deteriorated throughout the year. Allegations included government contracting to political party insiders and supporters. There continued to be questions regarding the transparency of government decisions to issue mineral and timber concession rights. There was a continuing widespread perception that officials used public power for private gain.

Civil society, media, and other nongovernmental parties particularly scrutinized and criticized the Ministries of Natural Resources, Public Works, Social Affairs, Justice and Police, Education, and Physical Planning, alleging widespread corruption and favoritism.

The Attorney General's Office showed a willingness to investigate claims of corruption throughout the year. In August 2015 the office launched a criminal investigation of officials of Energie Bedrijven Suriname (EBS), the state-owned electricity company, based on a report by the Central Government Accounting Office which identified numerous financial irregularities including payments for nondelivered goods and unauthorized contracting. Three persons were under investigation in this case. In August authorities announced the prosecution of one of the suspects.

In October the minister of justice and police reported that the bribery and arson investigations at the Alien Affairs Department, which began in September 2015, were unlikely to result in criminal charges. Initially the investigation targeted bribes allegedly taken for issuance of residency permits. Then, days after the minister dismissed all suspected staffers, an arsonist burned down the building housing the Alien Affairs Department, which was conducting the investigation.

Financial Disclosure: Officials were not subject to financial disclosure laws.

Public Access to Information: No law requires public disclosure of information. Although occasionally granted, access remained very limited in certain areas. There is a centralized office for media and information requests under the Office of the President. Gaps in official government statistics and bureaucratic hurdles made obtaining information difficult. There were no administrative or criminal sanctions for nondisclosure and no appeals mechanism.

Section 5. Governmental Attitude Regarding International and Nongovernmental Investigation of Alleged Violations of Human Rights

A number of independent domestic human rights groups generally operated without government restriction, investigating and publishing their findings on human rights cases. NGOs reported generally positive relationships with government officials, although officials were not always responsive to their views.

Government Human Rights Bodies: The Human Rights Office of the Ministry of Justice and Police is responsible for advising the government on regional and international proceedings against the state concerning human rights. It is also responsible for preparing the state's response to various international human rights reports. The National Assembly has a commission dealing with issues related to human rights.

Section 6. Discrimination, Societal Abuses, and Trafficking in Persons

Women

<u>Rape and Domestic Violence</u>: The law criminalizes rape, including spousal rape, and prescribes penalties for rape or forcible sexual assault of between 12 and 15 years' imprisonment and fines up to 100,000 Surinamese dollars (SRD) ($12,820). The government enforced the law effectively. Police received 218 reports of sexual abuse as of September. Authorities investigated and prosecuted all reported cases.

Violence against women remained a serious and pervasive problem. The law imposes sentences of four to eight years' imprisonment for domestic violence. Through September police received 870 reports of domestic abuse, down from 1,122 reports for the same period in 2015. Domestic abuse played a role in eight of the 27 homicides committed through September; prosecutions were pending.

The Victim Assistance Bureau of the Ministry of Justice and Police provided resources for victims of domestic violence and continued to raise awareness about domestic violence through public television programs. There were victims' rooms in police stations in Paramaribo and Nickerie. Authorities trained police units in dealing with survivors and perpetrators of sexual crimes and domestic violence. The Victim Assistance Bureau managed a shelter for female victims of domestic violence and children up to age 12 and served an average of 40 clients per year.

Authorities reported an average of 20 requests per week for restraining orders, primarily from women seeking protection from abusive partners. When granted, the restraining orders instruct the partners not to communicate with victims or otherwise contact them.

<u>Sexual Harassment</u>: There is no specific legislation on sexual harassment, but prosecutors cited various penal code articles in filing sexual harassment cases. There were no reported court cases involving sexual harassment in the workplace.

Stalking is a criminal offense, and police may investigate possible cases of stalking without the filing of a formal complaint. Pending investigation, police may issue temporary restraining orders limiting contact between victim and suspect for up to 30 days. If found guilty, offenders can receive prison sentences ranging from four to 12 years and fines from SRD 50,000 to 150,000 ($6,400 to $19,200).

<u>Reproductive Rights</u>: Couples and individuals have the right to decide the number, spacing, and timing of their children; manage their reproductive health; and have access to the information and means to do so free from discrimination, coercion, and violence. Access to information on modern contraception was widely available and, according to 2013 data from the UN Children's Fund (UNICEF), 47 percent of women ages 15-49 used modern contraceptive methods. Although more than 90 percent of births took place under the care of skilled health-care practitioners, the United Nations reported a maternal mortality rate of approximately 155 deaths per 100,000 live births. The causes for this high rate were primarily linked to pregnancy-induced hypertension (20 percent) and complications during labor and delivery (16 percent).

<u>Discrimination</u>: The law provides for protection of women's rights to equal access to education, employment, and property. Societal pressures and customs, especially in rural areas, inhibited the full exercise of these rights, particularly with respect to marriage and inheritance.

Men and women generally enjoy the same legal rights, but where citizens observed traditional local customs, these rights were somewhat infringed. The Bureau for Women and Children under the Ministry of Justice and Police was responsible for protecting the legal rights of women and children. Women experienced discrimination in access to employment and in rates of pay for the same or substantially similar work. The government did not undertake specific efforts to combat economic discrimination.

Children

<u>Birth Registration</u>: The 2014 amendment of the law on citizenship and residency provides that citizenship transmits to a child when either the father or mother has Surinamese citizenship at the time of birth, when the parent is Surinamese but has died before birth, or if the child is born in the country's territory and does not automatically acquire citizenship of another country. Births must be registered with the Civil Registry within one week. Failure to do so within the mandated period results in a more cumbersome process of registration through the Attorney General's Office.

<u>Child Abuse</u>: Physical and sexual abuse of children continued to be problems. Police registered 44 cases of physical abuse and 188 cases of child sexual abuse as of September, fewer than in the previous year. Observers believed the actual number of abuse cases was significantly higher than reported, since the office

handled only those cases reported to police. To avoid intimidation by perpetrators, there were arrangements for children to testify in special chambers at legal proceedings. The Youth Affairs Office continued to raise awareness about sexual abuse, drugs, and alcohol through a weekly television program. The government operated a "1-2-3" telephone hotline for children and provided confidential advice and aid to children in need. The hotline reported an average of 80 calls per day.

UNICEF continued cooperating with the government in providing training to officials from various ministries dealing with children and children's rights. The Ministry of Justice and Police opened child protection centers in Apoera and Coronie during the year to improve access to assistance for those wanting to report cases of child abuse and victims seeking counseling. If specialized services are needed, the centers reach out to other departments within the ministry, including the Bureau for Victim Care for counseling services.

Several cases of sexual exploitation, sexual and physical abuse, and neglect came to trial. Victims included both boys and girls. Sentences ranged up to 10 years in prison.

Early and Forced Marriage: Parental permission to marry is required until the age of 21. The marriage law sets the age of marital consent at 15 for girls and 17 for boys, provided parents of the parties agree to the marriage. Where local customs remain a strong influence on the family unit, girls traditionally marry at or near the legal age of consent.

Sexual Exploitation of Children: The law prohibits the commercial sexual exploitation of children, the sale of children, offering or procuring a child for child prostitution, and practices related to child pornography. Authorities prosecuted all reported violations. While the legal age of sexual consent is 14, trafficking-in-persons legislation makes sexual exploitation of a person under the age of 18 illegal. Criminal law penalizes persons responsible for recruiting children into prostitution and provides penalties of up to six years' imprisonment and a fine of SRD 100,000 ($12,800) for pimping. The law also prohibits child pornography, which carries a maximum penalty of six years' imprisonment and maximum fine of SRD 50,000 ($6,400). Violations are punishable by prison terms of up to 12 years.

Deteriorating economic circumstances led to an increasing number of adolescent boys and girls entering prostitution to support family or to pay for education. One NGO reported commercial sexual exploitation of children as young as 14. While not marked as a destination for child sex tourism, cases have been reported of tourists involved in child prostitution.

<u>Institutionalized Children</u>: A lack of financial support from the Ministry of Social Affairs for orphanages and other shelters for children significantly affected these institutions' ability to adequately take care of children.

<u>International Child Abductions</u>: The country is not a party to the 1980 Hague Convention on the Civil Aspects of Child Abduction. See the Department of State's *Annual Report on International Parental Child Abduction* at travel.state.gov/content/childabduction/en/legal/compliance.html.

Anti-Semitism

There was a declared Jewish community of approximately 150 persons. There were no reports of anti-Semitic acts or discrimination.

Trafficking in Persons

See the Department of State's *Trafficking in Persons Report* at www.state.gov/j/tip/rls/tiprpt/.

Persons with Disabilities

No laws prohibit discrimination against persons with physical or mental disabilities in employment, education, air travel and other transportation, access to the judicial system, or the provision of other state services. Persons with disabilities are eligible to receive general health benefits, but the process can be cumbersome. Persons with disabilities suffered from discrimination when applying for jobs and services. Authorities provided some training programs for persons with impaired vision or other disabilities. No laws or programs provide that persons with disabilities have access to buildings. A judge may rule to deny a person with a cognitive disability the right to vote, take part in business transactions, or sign legal agreements. Primary education was available for persons with disabilities and, depending on the disability, secondary and higher education could also be available. There was secondary and technical education for the deaf but not for the blind. No information was available regarding abuse in educational or institutional facilities for persons with disabilities. Persons with disabilities are eligible to receive a stipend from the government until they marry or turn 60. The Ministry of Social Affairs is responsible for protecting the rights of persons with disabilities.

Indigenous People

The law affords no special protection for, or recognition of, indigenous people. The IACHR identified the Maroons (descendants of escaped slaves who fled to the hinterland--approximately 22 percent of the population) as tribal peoples and thus entitled to the same rights as the indigenous Amerindian communities (approximately 4 percent of the population).

Maroons and Amerindians living in the remote and undeveloped interior had limited access to education, employment, and health and social services. Both groups participated in decisions affecting their tradition and culture, but they had limited influence in decisions affecting exploitation of energy, minerals, timber, and other natural resources on their lands. Both Maroons and Amerindians took part in regional governing bodies, as well as in the National Assembly, and were part of the governing coalition.

The government recognizes the different Maroon and indigenous tribes, but they hold no special status under national law, and there was no effective demarcation of their lands. Because authorities did not effectively demarcate or police Amerindian and Maroon lands, these populations continued to face problems with illegal and uncontrolled logging and mining. No laws grant indigenous people the right to share in the revenues from the exploitation of resources on their traditional lands. Organizations representing Maroon and Amerindian communities complained that small-scale mining operations, mainly by illegal gold miners, some of whom were themselves indigenous or supported by indigenous groups, dug trenches that cut residents off from their agricultural land and threatened to drive them away from their traditional settlements. Mercury runoff from these operations also contaminated sources of drinking water and threatened traditional food sources, especially freshwater fish.

Maroon and Amerindian groups complained about the government's granting of land within their traditional territories to third parties, who sometimes prevented the villages from engaging in their traditional activities on those lands. Maroon and Amerindian groups continued to cooperate with each other to exercise their rights more effectively. The Moiwana Human Rights Association, the Association of Indigenous Village Leaders (an umbrella group that represents the many smaller associations of indigenous persons), and other NGOs continued to promote the rights of indigenous people.

In November 2015 the Inter-American Court of Human Rights ruled against the government in the case of the Kalina and Lokono Peoples vs. Suriname. The case began in 2009, when the Kalina Indigenous Community of Maho filed a petition with the IACHR claiming that the government's granting of concessions to third parties for the exploitation of the land and natural resources the Maho community had occupied and used for centuries was a violation of their human rights. The petition claimed the encroachment on their territory negatively affected the development of the community. In 2014, despite the continuing litigation, the government continued to grant concession rights to third parties in the area of the Maho community. In 2014 the community reported that the government had issued a 49-acre concession to a third party.

The Inter-American Court declared the state responsible for violating the rights to recognition of juridical personality, to collective property, to political rights, and to cultural identity, and reminded the state of its duty to adopt appropriate domestic legal provisions. The court ruled that all the above had been prejudicial to the members of the Kalina and Lokono communities and ordered the government to legally recognize the Kalina and Lokono collective juridical personality; delimit, demarcate, and title the territory to the peoples; establish a community development fund; and rehabilitate areas affected by mining by third parties. At year's end the government had not taken action to carry out the court's orders.

Acts of Violence, Discrimination, and Other Abuses based on Sexual Orientation and Gender Identity

The constitution prohibits many forms of discrimination but does not address sexual orientation, gender identity, or HIV-positive status. Lesbian, gay, bisexual, transgender, and intersex (LGBTI) groups could associate freely, were very active, and advocated within society under the same laws that pertain to the assembly and association of other groups. In March 2015 the penal code was amended to include specific legislation regarding discrimination and hate speech based on sexual orientation, specifically protecting the LGBTI community. Violation of this law is punishable by a fine or prison sentence of up to one year. The legislation does not set standards for determining what constitutes such discrimination or hate speech. The law was in effect but had not been used in any case.

Despite the protective legislation, the LGBTI community faced discrimination from the government and society. The law specifies marriage as a union between a man and woman, making same-sex marriage illegal. The National Assembly and government openly discriminated against same-sex couples, as they were not recognized and were explicitly excluded from social security legislation passed in 2014. LGBTI persons, particularly transgender commercial sex workers, reported arbitrary arrests, harassment, and beatings by security forces. The police have no specific policy for handling of male transgender commercial sex workers, which resulted in those arrested being placed in male detention facilities where they faced harassment and other violence by other detainees.

There were few official reports of societal violence against LGBTI persons, primarily due to the victims' fear of retribution and because authorities reportedly did not take seriously complaints filed by members of the LGBTI community. There were reports of societal discrimination against the LGBTI community in areas of employment and housing.

At the recommendation of the UN's Universal Periodic Review, in August the Ministry of Justice and Police established a working group to make recommendations on actions to prevent and combat discrimination against the LGBTI community. The working group included representatives of the community.

HIV and AIDS Societal Stigma

Persons with HIV/AIDS continued to experience societal discrimination in employment and medical services. Medical treatment is free for HIV/AIDS patients covered under government insurance, but private insurers did not cover such treatment.

Other Societal Violence or Discrimination

Police statistics showed that crime in general was on the rise and had become more violent. Chinese shop owners continued to be targets of violent armed robberies, some of which resulted in fatalities. Violence in the gold-mining areas of the interior occurred primarily among and within the Brazilian and Maroon communities, where the government exercised little authority.

Section 7. Worker Rights

a. Freedom of Association and the Right to Collective Bargaining

The law provides for the right of workers to form and join unions of their choice without previous authorization or excessive requirements, the right to bargain collectively, and the right to strike. The law prohibits antiunion discrimination, requires that workers terminated for union activity be reinstated, and prohibits employer interference in union activities. Labor laws do not cover undocumented foreign workers.

While the government is effectively responsible for enforcing laws related to freedom of association and the right to collective bargaining, it was also the primary violator of the collective bargaining principles during the year. Collective bargaining agreements signed at different parastatals were violated when the government retracted its obligations under the agreements because they would violate the government's agreement with the International Monetary Fund. The government signed various labor agreements with different unions throughout the year, but it systematically failed to enforce these agreements. This led to strikes at government entities throughout the year. Penalties for violations of these rights range from six months' imprisonment, fines up to SRD 10,000 ($1,280), or both, and in cases of private entities, the penalties were generally sufficient to deter violations.

Workers formed and joined unions freely and exercised their right to strike. In September the government threatened to fire workers of the state-owned electricity company EBS who were striking to demand implementation of a collective bargaining agreement signed with government representatives. The employees later came to an agreement over compensation and returned to work.

Some trade union leaders held high-level positions in the coalition government, while another trade union was associated with a party in the opposition.

In isolated cases private employers refused to bargain or recognize collective bargaining rights, but the unions usually pressured the employers to negotiate. There were some reports that companies exploited legislative gaps and hired more contract employees than direct-hire staff to perform core business functions in order to cut costs.

b. Prohibition of Forced or Compulsory Labor

The law prohibits all forms of forced or compulsory labor. By law administrative penalties for violations are up to six months' imprisonment, a fine up to SRD 500,000 ($64,000), or both. Criminal penalties for violations range from five to 20 years' imprisonment. Labor inspectors received training on detecting forced labor, but no data were available on inspection efforts specific to forced labor, and there were no cases during the year.

Also, see the Department of State's *Trafficking in Persons Report* at www.state.gov/j/tip/rls/tiprpt/.

c. Prohibition of Child Labor and Minimum Age for Employment

The law sets the minimum age for most types of employment at 14 and restricts working hours for minors to day shifts, but it does not limit the number of hours minors can work. The law permits children younger than 14 to work only in a family-owned business, small-scale agriculture, and special vocational work. It prohibits children younger than 18 from doing hazardous work, defined as work dangerous to life, health, and decency. The law does not permit children under the age of 15 to work on boats. Authorities may prosecute parents who permit their children to work in violation of labor laws. Employing a child under 14 is punishable by fines and up to 12 months' imprisonment. While such penalties generally were sufficient to deter violations, authorities rarely enforced them, typically responding only when a report was filed.

The Ministry of Labor's Department of Labor Inspection did not identify any cases of child labor in the formal business sector during the year. The police are responsible for enforcement in the informal sector and enforced the minimum working age law sporadically. Resources also remained inadequate.

Child labor remained a problem in the informal sector and, according to newspaper reports, grew during the year due to deteriorating economic circumstances in the country. The government lacked resources to carry out a survey quantifying child labor. Historically, child labor occurred in agriculture, logging, fisheries, and the construction sector, as well as in street vending. Isolated cases of child labor occurred in the informal gold-mining sector in the interior and in commercial sexual exploitation (see also section 6, Children).

Also see the Department of Labor's *Findings on the Worst Forms of Child Labor* www.dol.gov/ilab/reports/child-labor/findings/.

d. Discrimination with Respect to Employment and Occupation

The constitution prohibits many kinds of discrimination, but enforcement was selective. Discrimination in employment reportedly occurred with regard to disability, gender, sexual orientation, gender identity, and HIV/AIDS status.

e. Acceptable Conditions of Work

A minimum wage law went into effect in January 2015. It set the lowest wage as of January 2016 at SRD 5.22 ($0.67) per hour or SRD 835 ($107) per month. Beginning January 2017, the hourly wage was scheduled to increase to SRD 6.14 ($0.79) per hour. The intent of the law, which was to improve worker pay conditions, was undermined by a significant devaluation of the Surinamese dollar during the year.

Government employees constituted approximately 40 percent of the estimated 125,000-member formal-sector workforce and frequently supplemented their salaries with second or third jobs, often in the informal sector.

Work in excess of 45 hours per week on a regular basis requires special government permission, which was routinely granted. The law requires premium pay for such overtime work, prohibits excessive overtime, requires a 24-hour rest period per week, and stipulates paid annual holidays. Overtime is generally limited to four hours per day, for a maximum 12-hour workday. During the holiday season, the retail sector has a blanket permit allowing for work up to 15 hours a day, including seven hours of overtime. The government sets occupational health and safety standards, which generally are current and appropriate for the main industries in the country.

Laws were effectively enforced only in the formal sectors. Ten to 12 inspectors in the Occupational Health and Safety Division of the Ministry of Labor are responsible for enforcing occupational safety and health regulations, but they did not make regular occupational safety and health inspections. The Department of Labor Inspection, with approximately 63 inspectors, is responsible for enforcing labor laws. Penalties for violating the labor laws vary from fines to suspension of business licenses, depending on the severity of the case, and were sufficient to deter the worst violations.

In 2014 a summary law system was introduced for labor law violations in the formal sector, which makes it possible for prosecutors to levy fines when labor violations are identified. The Prosecutors' Office deputized labor inspectors to implement the system and levy fines as determined by law. If the accused refuses to pay these fines, or disputes these fines, the case can be brought before a judge for a quick ruling.

A significant number of persons worked in the informal economy, where there was limited enforcement of labor laws. Workers in the informal sector, particularly in small-scale mining, often were exposed to dangerous conditions and hazardous substances such as mercury.

Limited data were available on workplace accidents. The International Labor Organization, however, noted an increasing number of serious or fatal occupational accidents, as well as steps by labor inspectors to begin occupational safety and health training in mines, construction, and public service. The majority of fatal occupational accidents took place in the mining sector.

Workers in the formal sector can remove themselves from situations that endanger health or safety without jeopardy to their employment, and authorities effectively protected employees in this situation. Workers in the informal sector did not enjoy the same protection.